Content

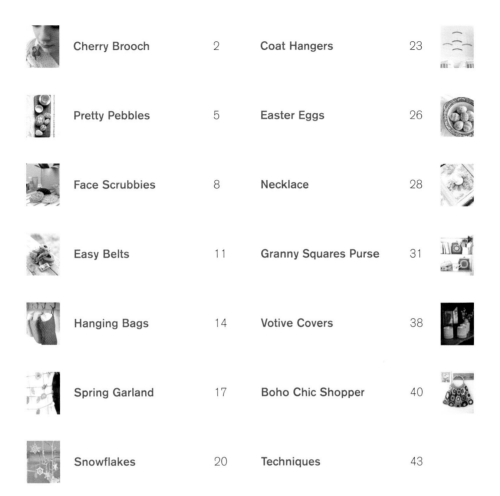

Introduction

These clever little projects are a great way to use up leftover yarn while making a range of useful and attractive items for the home or lovely handmade gifts. From stylish votive covers to face scrubbies and stunning snowflakes, you'll find plenty of crocheting projects to choose from for stashbusting success.

Each project has clear instructions and colour photographs or diagrams to help you achieve perfect results. You can follow them to the letter or use them as a basis for your own creations. In addition, a handy techniques section explains all the basic skills needed, and most projects are suitable for experienced crocheters and novices alike. All projects are small and portable, so they're perfect for crocheting when you're on the move. We're sure you'll enjoy making them.

Cherry Brooch

This striking brooch is an excellent project on which to start practising the basic crochet stitches described on pages 43–5. Quirky and bright, this splash of colour is sure to make you stand out in a crowd.

MATERIALS

- Oddments of 4-ply yarn in red (A) and green (B)
- 2.5mm (UK12:USC/2) crochet hook
- Tapestry needle
- Toy filling
- Brooch bar

CHERRY (make 2)

Using 2.5mm hook and A, make 4 ch and join with a sl st to form a ring.

Round 1: Make 1 ch (this does not count as a st). Into the circle work 7 dc.

Round 2: Work 2 dc into each dc worked into the circle. You should now have 14 sts. You can see that as you work each step, or round of sts, a ring is formed in your crochet (**image 1**).

Round 3: Work 1 dc into each dc st made in Round 2.

Round 4: *Work 2 dc into the next dc then 1 dc into the next dc; rep from * 6 more times so you have 21 sts.

Round 5: Work 1 dc into each of the 21 dc.

Fasten off, leaving a long length of yarn. Thread the end onto a tapestry needle and work running stitches around the edge. Stuff the cherry with toy filling and gather up the sts to close (**image 2**). Fasten off and sew the end of yarn into the cherry to prevent the sts unravelling.

Repeat to make one more cherry.

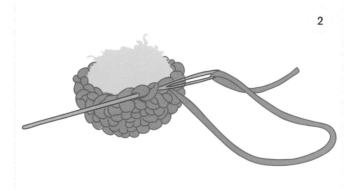

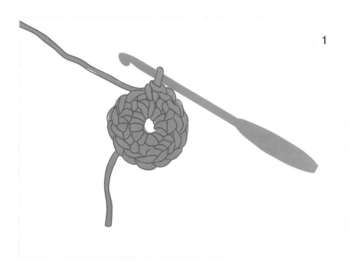

TIP

As you pull the yarn through each loop for each stitch, you are holding on to the other end of the yarn. It matters how tightly or loosely you hold that yarn. You need to keep it consistent, or you'll get a piece that has rows which are super-tight or super-stretched. Watch out for this: it can make your work come out wonky, even if you crochet the right number of stitches.

LEAF (make 2)

Using 2.5mm hook and B, make 6 ch and join with a sl st to form a ring.

Round 1: 1 ch (this does not count as a stitch). Into the circle work 2 dc, 5 tr and 2 dc (**image 3**).

Round 2: Work 1 dc into each of the first 2 sts; work 2 dc into the next st; work 2 tr into the next st; work 3 tr into the next st; work 2 tr into the next st; work 2 dc into the next st and 1 dc into each of the last 2 sts.

Next Round: Sl st to the next st then work 5 ch to form the stalks before fastening off, leaving a long length of yarn with which to sew the cherries onto the ends (**image 4**).

Make one more leaf.

To finish off, sew the leaves together at the point where the stalk begins. Stitch a brooch bar across the back of the leaves and sew in loose ends to prevent the work from coming undone.

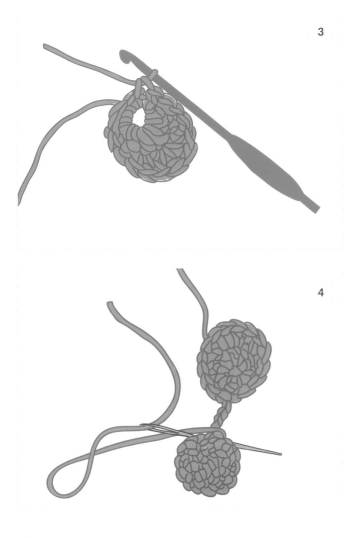

3

4

Pretty Pebbles

These decorated pebbles make ideal paperweights, and also look lovely as table decorations or placed in baskets around the home. The inspiration for these designs came from old tablemats, and you can adapt the designs if you have similar items to hand.

MATERIALS
- 25g ball of No. 12 crochet or embroidery thread
- 2.5mm (UK12:USC/2) crochet hook
- Smooth stones, approx 2½–4in (6–10cm) in diameter
- Scissors

SEA URCHIN DESIGN

Using 2.5mm hook, make 10 ch and join with a sl st to form a ring.

Round 1: Into the ring work 18 dc.

Round 2: *Work 2 tr into first dc, 2 ch, miss 2 sts; rep from * 6 times (**image 1**).

Round 3: * Work 2 tr into first dc, miss next dc, 4 ch; rep from * 6 times.

Round 4: *Work 2 tr into first dc, miss next dc, 6 ch; rep from * 6 times.

Round 5: *Work 2 tr into first dc, miss next dc, 8 ch; rep from * 6 times.

Cont in this way, working 2 extra ch in each group so that the circle diameter increases. When the work measures slightly more than the stone, you are ready to start shaping it to fit round the pebble.

Next Round: Work the same pattern but reduce the number of ch sts in each group by 3.

Foll Round: Repeat as necessary.

Your work should now be curving into a dome shape (**image 2**). Once the chain stitch count is down to 8 sts or 6 sts and the stone fits inside, you can complete the crocheted pebble as follows:

Next Round: *Make 4 dc into the space of each chain section and 1 dc into the first dc, miss next dc; rep from* 6 times.

The rest of the pattern is worked with the stone inside. Dc into every second st all the way round, pulling the work tight around the stone. For the final round dc into every second st again to the end of the round. Pull the thread through the last st, pull tight and cut the thread.

NET DESIGN

Using 2.5mm hook, make 10 ch and join with a sl st to form a ring.

Round 1: Into the ring work 18 dc.

Round 2: *Work 2 tr into first dc, 2 ch, miss 2 sts; rep from * 6 times. This round is complete.

Round 3: *7 ch, 1 dc into sp; rep from * 6 times.

Round 4: *8 ch, 1 dc into sp; rep from * 6 times.

Round 5: *9 ch, 1 dc into sp; rep from * 6 times.

Cont in this way, working 1 extra ch in each round until your work measures slightly larger than your stone.

Next Round: To shape your work into a dome to fit over the stone, *4 dc into each sp, 1 dc into next st; repeat from * 6 times.

The rest of the pattern is worked with the stone inside (**image 3**). Dc into every second st all the way round, pulling the work tight around the stone. For the final round dc into every second st again to the end of the round. Pull the thread through the last st, pull tight and cut the thread.

SPIRAL DESIGN

Using 2.5mm hook, make 6 ch and join with a sl st to form a ring.

Round 1: *6 ch, 1 dc into the ring; rep from * 6 times.

Round 2: *4 ch, 1 dc into the next loop; rep from * 6 times.

Round 3: *4 ch, 2 dc into the next loop, 1 dc into the next dc; rep from * 6 times.

Round 4: *4 ch, 2 dc into the next loop, 1 dc into each of the first dc of the group; rep from * 6 times.

Round 5: *4 ch, 2 dc into the next loop, 1 dc in each of the first 3 dc of the group; rep from * 6 times.

Cont in this way, working 1 extra dc in each group on each round until your work measures slightly larger than your stone.

The rest of the pattern is worked with the stone inside. Dc into every second st all the way round, pulling the work tight around the stone. For the final round, dc into every second st again to the end of the round. Pull the thread through the last st, pull tight and cut the thread.

Face Scrubbies

MATERIALS

- Oddments of DK yarn (we used a salmon-pink smooth acrylic for 'Lovely to Use'; a lilac short-eyelash acrylic for 'Clearing it Away' and a purple acrylic chenille for the 'Feel Good' scrubbie)
- 5mm (UK6:USH/8) crochet hook
- Tapestry needle
- Acrylic wadding (for the 'Feel Good' scrubbie)

Hand-crocheted face scrubbies are the perfect addition to your skin-care routine. Ideally the yarn should not contain animal fibres because they may not be suitable for sensitive skin; all kinds of plant- and oil-based yarns are good.

'LOVELY TO USE' SCRUBBIE:

Front

Using 5mm hook and a smooth acrylic DK, make 3 ch. If your slip knot tightened from the short end, work Round 1 directly into the top loop of the first ch made (**image 1**). Otherwise join with a sl st, make 1 ch, then work Round 1 into the ring.

Round 1: 6 dc, join with a sl st into ch. 1 ch, turn work.

Round 2: 1 dtr in same place as turning ch, *(1 dc, 1 dtr in next st. The tall st should go to the back of the work – see **image 2**), rep from * to end, join with a sl st, 1 ch, turn work (7 bobbles).

Round 3: 1 dc in same place as turning ch, *1 dc, (2 dc in next st), rep from * to last st, 1 dc in last st, join with a sl st,1 ch, turn work (21 sts).

Round 4: 1 dtr in same place as turning ch, *1 dc, (1 dc, 1 dtr in next st), rep from * to end, join with a sl st, 1 ch, turn work (10 bobbles).

Round 5: *2 dc in dtr, 2 dc, rep from *to end, join with a sl st (**image 3**). Fasten off.

Back and finger bar

Make 3 ch and join with a sl st to form a ring.

Round 1: 1 ch, 6 dc in ring, join with a sl st, turn work.

Round 2: 1 ch, 1 dc in same place, 2 dc in each st to end, join with a sl st, turn work (14 sts).

Round 3: 1 ch, 1 dc in same place, *1 dc, (2 dc in next st), rep from * to end, join with a sl st, turn work.

Round 4: 1 ch, 1 dc in same place, *2 dc, (2 dc in next st), rep from * to end, join with a sl st, turn work.

Round 5: 1 ch, 1 dc in same place, *3 dc, (2 dc in next st), rep from * to end, join with a sl st, turn work (35 sts).

Do not break off yarn, cont to make finger bar (**image 4**).

Row 1: 1 ch, 1 dc in same place, 1 dc.

Rep this row approximately 14 times to length of diameter of the back.

To finish

Position WS of back and front together with the finger bar loose., then position last row of finger bar exactly opposite to where it began. Join using dc (1 dc through the finger bar, the back and the front) three times, dc in each stitch all round. Fasten off.

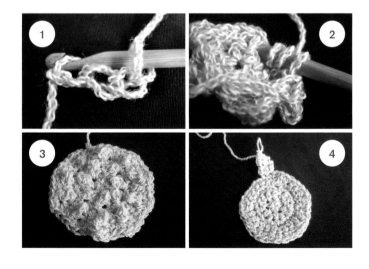

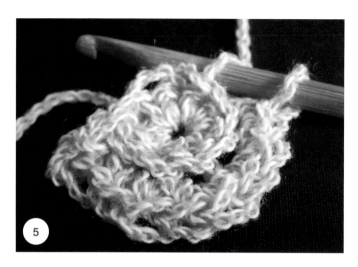

'CLEARING IT AWAY' SCRUBBIE
Front

Using 5mm hook and a short eyelash acrylic DK, make 3 ch, join with a sl st to form a ring. This yarn is not easy to work with but does the trick of clearing away any dead skin cells.

Work all dc in back loop only of each st to give a ridge (see photo inserting hook into back loop only: **image 5**).

Round 1: 1 ch, 6 dc in ring, join with a sl st, turn work.

Round 2: 1 ch, 1 dc in same place, 2 dc in back loop of next st to end, join with 1 sl st, turn work (14 sts).

Round 3: 1 ch, 1 dc in same place, *1 dc in back loop, 2 dc in back loop of next st, rep from * to end, join with a sl st, turn work.

Round 4: 1 ch, 1 dc in same place, *2 dc in back loop, 2 dc in back loop of next st, rep from * to end, join with a sl st, turn work.

Round 5: 1 ch, 1 dc in same place, *3 dc in back loop, 2 dc in back loop of next st, rep from * to end, join with a sl st, turn work (35 sts). Fasten off.

Work a back and finger bar and complete as 'Lovely to Use'.

'FEEL GOOD' SCRUBBIE
Front

Using 5mm hook and an acrylic chenille in DK thickness, make 3 ch, join with a sl st to form a ring. Do not turn work on each round: one side will be smoother. The smooth side will be the RS.

Round 1: 1 ch, 6 dc in ring, join with a sl st.

Round 2: 1 ch, 1 dc in same place, 2 dc in each st to end, join with a sl st (14 sts).

Round 3: 1 ch, 1 dc in same place, *1 dc, 2 dc in next st, rep from * to end, join with a sl st.

Round 4: 1 ch, 1 dc in same place, *2 dc, 2 dc in next st, rep from * to end, join with a sl st.

Round 5: 1 ch, 1 dc in same place, *3 dc, 2 dc in next st, rep from * to end, join with a sl st (35 sts).

Work a back and finger bar and complete as 'Lovely to Use'. As this can be used dry to exfoliate the face, instead of making a flat scrubbie fill the space between the two pieces with acrylic wadding to make it into a pad.

Easy Belts

Accessorize your outfits with beautiful crochet belts. These simple striped belts are ideal for using up linen or cotton yarn scraps, and you can try out various ratios of colours and stripes to create your own unique designs. Tension is important here, so follow the instructions for the sample first before making a belt.

MATERIALS

- Rowan Creative Linen, 50% linen, 50% cotton (approx 218yd/200m per 100g skein):
  1 x skein in 621 Natural (A)
- Scraps of linen/cotton yarns.
  We used Rowan Creative Linen:
  623 Dusk (B), 625 Teal (C), 627 Salmon (D), 632 Leaf (E), 638 Eggplant (F)
- 3mm (US11:US-) crochet hook
- 1½in (4cm) mottled beige slide buckle
- 2 x 35mm D-rings
- Tapestry needle
- Measuring tape

TENSION SAMPLE

Using 3mm hook, make a foundation chain of 21 sts. *1 ch, insert your hook through the second st from the needle and dc 1 row (20 sts). Rep from * until 6 rows completed. Hold a measuring tape over your sample and count how many sts equate to 2in (5cm). Use this number to calculate the number of sts you need for your foundation chains. Numbers of sts quoted in patterns equate to 11 sts = 2in (5cm) using 3mm hook to fit a 30in (75cm) waist.

FRINGED BELT

Using 3mm hook and A, make a foundation chain of 167 sts.

Row 1: 1 ch, working into second st from hook, dc into each st to end.

Rows 2–4: 1 ch, dc into each st to end.

Row 5: 1 ch, dc into next 3 sts, *work 3 tr into gap below next st, take hook out of working loop, insert it into the top of the first of these 3 tr, pick up working loop again and draw through top of first tr to close the group of sts, dc into next 3 sts. Rep from * to end.

Rows 6–8: As rows 2–4.

Cut yarn to 2¾in (7cm) and pull through final loop and finish off using tapestry needle.

Join yarn at the top corner of one end and work 70 ch.

Cut yarn to 2¾in (7cm) and pull through final loop. Finish off with a tapestry needle by running it back through the foundation chain (**image 1**). Repeat, making 7–9 fringes along each end.

1

BUCKLE BELT

Using 3mm hook and C, make a foundation chain of 215 sts.

Row 1: 1 ch, working into second st from hook, dc into each st to end.

Rows 2–3: 1 ch, dc into each st to end.

Row 4: Using B, 1 ch, dc into each st to end.

Row 5: Using E, 1 ch, dc into each st to end.

Row 6: Using A, 1 ch, dc into next 3 sts, *tr into the gap below the next st, dc into next 3 sts. Rep from * to end.

Row 7: 1 ch, dc into each st to end.

Row 8: Using B, 1 ch, dc into each st to end.

Cut yarn to 12in (30cm) and pull through final loop and finish off using tapestry needle.

Finish off all other yarn ends, leaving the 12in (30cm) long final yarn in B to secure the belt buckle.

Thread one end of the belt through the buckle. Turn over and fold the belt back on itself. Using a tapestry needle and the remaining long yarn end, use a tight backstitch or overstitch to secure the buckle (**image 2**).

JEANS BELT

Using 3mm hook and B, make a foundation chain of 167 sts.

Row 1: 1 ch, working into 2nd st from hook, dc into each st to end.

Row 2: Using F, 1 ch, dc into each st to end.

Row 3: Using D, 1 ch, dc into next 3 sts, *tr into the gap below the next st, dc into next 3 sts. Repeat from * to end.

Cut yarn to leave a 12in (30cm) end. Finish off all other yarn ends with a tapestry needle, leaving the 12in (30cm) long final yarn in D to secure the D-rings.

This creates a narrow strip making half your belt. Rep rows 1–3 to make the second half. This time, do not cut Yarn D until you have used it to join the two halves together with a crochet seam (**image 3**).

Thread one end of your belt through both D-rings. Turn over and fold the belt back on itself. Using a tapestry needle and the remaining long yarn end in D, use a tight backstitch or over stitch to secure the D-rings ⅜in (1cm) apart with two parallel lines of stitching (**image 4**).

TIP
To make a crochet seam, hold the two pieces to be joined right sides facing. Join them by working line of double crochet (dc) along the edge, inserting the hook through both layers of crochet for each dc stitch. See also page 47.

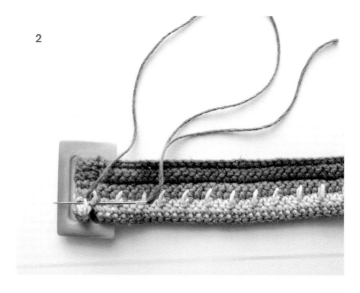

Hanging Bags

MATERIALS
- Rowan Handknit 100% cotton,
  (93yd/85m per 50g ball):
  2 balls in 350 Florence (A)
  2 balls in 349 Ochre (B)
  2 balls in 358 Pacific (C)
- 3.5mm (UK9:USE/4) and 5mm
  (UK6:USH/8) crochet hooks

Clear up your clutter and create these stylish bags to hang around your home. They provide great portable storage for everyday essentials.

SIZE
Approx 8½in (22cm) in diameter and 9½in (25cm) deep.

SPECIAL ABBREVIATIONS
Beg cl (begin cluster): Make 3 ch (counts as 1 tr), (yrh and insert hook through st, yrh and draw loop through, yrh and draw through first 2 loops) twice, yrh and draw through all 3 loops on hook.
Cl (cluster): (Yrh and insert hook through st, yrh and draw loop through, yrh and draw through first 2 loops) three times, yrh and draw through all 4 loops on hook.

BASE (all baskets)
Round 1: Using 3.5mm hook and A, B or C, make 6 ch and join with sl st to form a ring.
Round 2: 3 ch (counts as 1 tr), 1 tr into same place, 2 tr into each tr of previous round, join with sl st into third of 3 ch (32 tr).
Round 3: 3 ch (counts as 1 tr), 1 tr into same place, * (1 tr into next tr, 2 tr into next tr); rep from * to last tr, 1 tr into last tr, join with sl st into third of 3 ch (48 tr).
Round 4: 3 ch (counts as 1 tr), 1 tr into same place, * (1 tr into each of next 2 tr, 2 tr into next tr); rep from * to last 2 tr, 1 tr into each of last 2 tr, join with sl st into third of 3 ch (64 tr).
Round 5: 3 ch (counts as 1 tr), 1 tr into every tr from previous round, join with sl st into third of 3 ch (64 tr). Base is completed.

ORANGE BASKET (A)
Round 1: 3 ch (counts as 1 tr), beg cl into next tr, 1 ch, *miss 1 tr, 1 cl in next tr, 1 ch; rep from * to end, join with sl st to ch at top of beg cl (32 clusters).
Round 2: 3 ch, beg cl into next 1 ch sp, 1 ch, 1 cl in next 1 ch sp, 1 ch; rep from * to end, join with sl st to ch at top of beg cl. Rep this round 15 times more.

Rim

1 dc into next tr (mark this st), 1 dc into every tr to end of round. When you reach the marker, do not join the round. Simply remove the marker and work the marked st. Replace the marker in the new st, so that you know where the new round begins. Work a further two rounds in this way. Fasten off.

Loop

Weave in any loose ends. Using 5mm hook and yarn doubled attach yarn to back of basket (this will be where the rounds have been joined) with a sl st. Make 10 ch and then rejoin to basket with a sl st. Fasten off.

OCHRE BASKET (B)

Round 1: 3 ch (counts as 1 tr), 1 tr in next tr, *miss 1 tr, 2 tr in next tr; rep from * to end, join with sl st to third of 3 ch (32 pairs).
Round 2: Sl st between 3 ch and first tr, 3 ch (counts as 1 tr) 1 tr in same place, * miss next 2 tr and work 2 tr between next 2 sts; rep from * to end, join with sl st to third of 3 ch (32 pairs). Rep this round 19 more times. Complete by working Rim and Loop.

BLUE BASKET (C)

Round 1: 3 ch (counts as 1 tr), *miss next tr, 1 tr in next tr, 1 tr in the missed tr (crossed tr made); rep from * to last st, 1 tr in last tr, join with sl st to third of 3 ch (31 crossed tr and 2tr).
Round 2: Sl st into next tr, 3 ch (counts as 1 tr), *miss next tr, 1 tr in next tr, 1 tr in the missed tr (crossed tr made); repeat from * to last st, 1 tr in last tr, join with sl st to third of 3 ch. Rep this round 19 times more. Complete by working Rim and Loop.

Spring Garland

MATERIALS

- Cotton knitting yarns (dark and light green, dark and light yellow, natural, pale blue)
- 3.5mm (UK9:USE/4) crochet hook
- Fine dark embroidery cotton (for butterfly bodies and antennae)
- Tapestry needle
- Scissors
- Spray starch
- Iron

Bring springtime into your home with this simple and pretty garland. Brighten up a banister or mantelpiece, drape around a bookcase, or use as a curtain tie-back.

CHAIN (MAKE 1)

Using green cotton yarn, crochet a simple chain approximately 60in (1.5m) long. Make a loop with the tails of the cotton at both ends.

LEAVES (MAKE 14)

5 ch, dc in second chain from hook, 1 htr in next, 1 dc in next, work (2 htr in last, 2 ch, dc in second ch from hook, 2 htr) in last ch. Working now on the opposite side of foundation ch, 1 dc in next, 1 htr in next, dc in last.
Fasten off with sl st in the first dc of round (**image 1**).

1

TIP

Make a garland to celebrate every season. There's plenty of inspiration online, but to start with you could try leaves, acorns and pumpkins for autumn; snowflakes, berries and fir trees for winter and strawberries, roses and bees for summer.

PRIMROSES (MAKE 11)

6 ch, sl st into first ch to form a ring.

Round 1: Change colour, 1 ch, 1 tr into next st, *2 tr into next st; rep from * into next 4 sts, sl st into first st to complete round.

Round 2: Change colour, 1 ch, *3 tr into next st, 1 ch, sl st into next st, 1 ch ; rep from * until 5 petals completed, 3 tr into next st, 1 ch, sl st into next st, cutting the yarn to approx 2in (5cm) and pulling it all the way through.

Finish off all ends with a tapestry needle (**image 2**).

BUTTERFLIES (MAKE 6):

4 ch, sl st into first ch to form a ring.

4 ch, work 3 dtr (double treble) into ring, 6 ch, sl st into ring, 6 ch, work 3 dtr into ring, 4 ch, sl st into ring, 3 ch, work 2 tr into ring, 4 ch, sl st into ring, 4 ch, work 2 tr into ring, 3 ch, sl st into ring, cutting the yarn to 2in (5cm) and pulling it all the way through on the last sl st (**image 3**). Use a darning needle to stitch a body and antennae onto each butterfly with a length of the fine dark embroidery cotton.

TO FINISH OFF

Sew in any remaining loose ends. Following the instructions on the can, starch and press the pieces with a hot iron. Lay the crochet chain out, and arrange the pieces along its length. Using a tapestry needle, attach all the pieces to the chain (**image 4**).

2

3

4

Snowflakes

MATERIALS

- Cotton crochet thread No. 5 in blue, pink and lemon
- 2mm (UK14:USB/2) crochet hook
- Embroidery needle
- Scissors
- Liquid starch
- Resealable plastic bag
- Old towel
- Polyboard/foamboard
- Pins
- Silver/grey embroidery floss

Ensure a white Christmas (or pastel, if you prefer) with dainty crochet snowflakes. You will need a lot of pins to pin out the points of the snowflakes, so that you get the shapes right.

BLUE SNOWFLAKE

Using 2mm hook, work 6 ch. Join with a sl st to form a ring.

Round 1: 10 ch, (1 tr into ring, 7 ch) 5 times.
Join with sl st to third ch in first 10 ch.

Round 2: 1 dc into sl st at the end of Round 1 (4 ch, 1 dc into same st, 3 ch, miss 3 ch, 1 htr in next st [i.e. fourth of 7 ch], 3 ch, sl st in third ch from hook, 1 htr into same st as last htr, 3 ch, miss next 3 ch, 1 dc into top of tr in Round 1) 6 times, join with a sl st to first dc.
Fasten off.
Finish off ends by threading onto an embroidery needle and running through sts at the back of your work.

PINK SNOWFLAKE

Work 6 ch, join with a sl st to form a ring.

Round 1: (15 ch, sl st into ring), 5 times, 12 ch, 1 tr into ring.

Round 2: *9 ch, sl st in second ch from hook and in next 2 ch, 5 ch, sl st into second ch from hook and in next ch, 6 ch, sl st in fifth ch from hook and in next ch, 3 ch, sl st in second ch from hook and next ch, sl st in rem 2 ch from previous 5 ch, 4 ch, sl st in second ch from hook and in next 2 ch, sl st in rem 5 ch from previous 9 ch, sl st in third ch of next loop from Round 1, 4 ch, miss next 4 ch of loop (1 tr, 5 ch, 1 tr) in next ch, 4 ch, miss next 4 ch of loop, sl st into next ch rep from * 5 more times, ending last repeat with the sl st into the top of the tr from the end of round 1 to join.
Finish off ends by threading onto an embroidery needle and running through sts at the back of your work.

LEMON SNOWFLAKE

Work 6 ch and join with a sl st to form a ring.

Round 1: 6 ch, 1dc in ring, 5 ch, sl st in second ch from hook, (3 ch, sl st in second ch from hook) twice, 1 ch, miss next ch of previous 5 ch, sl st in next ch, 1ch, *(1 dc, 3 ch, 1dc) in ring, 5 ch, sl st in second ch from hook, (3 ch, sl st in second ch from hook) twice, 1 ch, miss next ch of previous 5 ch, sl st in next ch, 1ch, rep from * 4 times, 1 dc, 3 ch, sl st into third ch of first 6 ch to join. Finish off ends by threading onto an embroidery needle and running through sts at the back of your work and snipping off the ends.

TO FINISH OFF

Wash all pieces using mild soap in warm water. Rinse thoroughly and rinse and roll out in a towel to remove excess water.

Lay out flat and leave to dry thoroughly.

Pour neat liquid stiffener into a resealable plastic bag.

Put your dry crochet pieces in, remove as much air as possible before sealing the bag and work the stiffener into each piece fully with your hands. You may need to do a batch at a time, depending on how prolific you've been.

Remove the snowflakes from the stiffener, squeezing to remove excess liquid. Take your time to pin out each one as geometrically as possible on a sheet of polyboard and leave to dry thoroughly.

Thread a long length of silver/grey embroidery floss through each snowflake so you can hang them up.

Coat Hangers

Pretty up plain hangers with crochet to keep your clothes and wardrobe looking their best.

MATERIALS
- DK cotton yarn in two colours (A and B)
- 4mm (UK8:USG/6) crochet hook
- Scissors

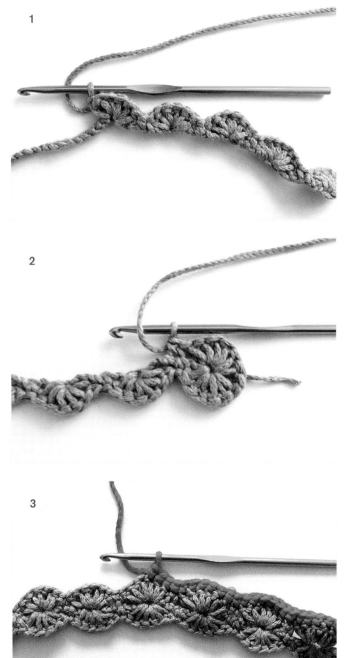

SIZE
All instructions are to fit a standard plain 16½in (42cm) wooden coat hanger.

FRONT
Using 4mm crochet hook and A, make 112 ch.

Round 1: 5 dtr into fourth ch from hook, *miss next 3 ch, dc into next ch, miss next 3 ch, 6 dtr into next ch; repeat from * ending with 1 sl st in last ch, turn (14 half shells: **image 1**).

Round 2: Working on the opposite side of the starting ch, * 6 dtr into centre bottom of previous half shell, dc in bottom of previous dc (**image 2**); repeat from * to end of row, sl st into last ch to complete the final shell.
Fasten off.

Round 3: Using B, dc in each st around, sl st into first stitch to complete and fasten off (**image 3**).

BACK
Repeat instructions for front, but do not fasten off yarn B at the end of round 3.

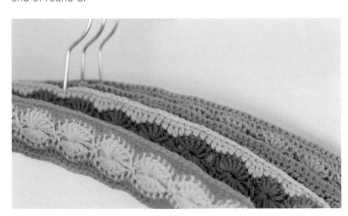

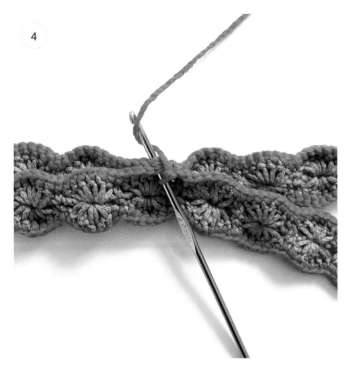

TO FINISH OFF

Lay the front and back pieces together. Starting halfway along, i.e. between shells seven and eight, using yarn B, and working through the sts of the front and back sections at the same time to join the two, dc in every dc around one end and along the bottom edge to the other end (**image 4**). Insert the coat hanger and continue to close the front and back pieces with dc, encasing the hanger as you go until you reach the hook (**image 5**).

Finish off yarn and hide the end of it by hooking it through to the inside of the coat hanger cover.

TIP

These brilliant stash-busters not only tart up tatty old hangers but will also help prevent your clothes from slipping off them.

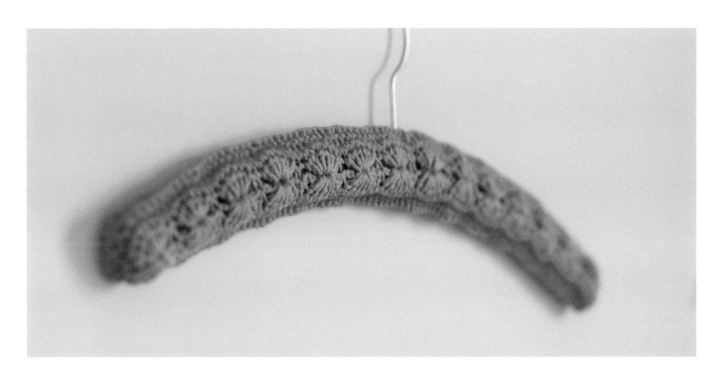

Easter Eggs

Don't let sugary treats rule the roost at Easter; let your creative side take over with some snazzy springtime crochet instead!

MATERIALS

- 1 x 50g ball of white cotton DK yarn
- Scraps of blue embroidery threads in three different shades from light to dark
- 4mm (UK8:USG/6) crochet hook
- Stitch marker
- Hollowfibre or cotton stuffing
- Tapestry needle

PATTERN NOTE

These instructions are for a plain egg. Use various amounts of blue embroidery threads with the white cotton to create speckled variegated tones and stripes. Simply cut a length of embroidery thread and crochet doubled with the DK cotton.

Using 4mm hook, make 2 ch (counts as a st), dc 5 into second ch from hook, sl st into first st (6 sts).
Mark end of round with a stitch marker.

Round 1: 2 dc into each st to end of round (12 sts).
Round 2: 1 dc into each st to end of round (12 sts).
Round 3: *1 dc into first st, 2 dc into next st, rep from * to end of round (18 sts).
Round 4: 1 dc into each st to end of round (18 sts).
Round 5: *1 dc into next 2 sts, 2 dc into next st, rep from * to end of round (24 sts).
Round 6: 1 dc into each st to end of round (24 sts).
Round 7: *1 dc into next 3 sts, 2 dc into next st, rep from * to end of round (30 sts).
Round 8: 1 dc into each st to end of round (30 sts).
Round 9: 1 dc into each st to end of round (30 sts).
Round 10: 1 dc into each st to end of round (30 sts).
Round 11: *1 dc into next 4 sts, miss the next st, rep from * to end of round (24 sts).
Round 12: 1 dc into each st to end of round (24 sts).
Round 13: *1 dc into next 3 sts, miss the next st, rep from * to end of round (18 sts).
Round 14: *1 dc into next 2 sts, miss the next st, rep from * to end of round (12 sts).
Stuff firmly.
Round 15: *1 dc into next st, miss the next st, rep from * to end of round (6 sts).
Hook the thread through all remaining stitches and tie off.
Darn in end.

Necklace

This pretty crocheted necklace is a stylish accessory for both day and evening wear.

MATERIALS

- Rowan Panama, 55% viscose, 33% cotton, 12% linen (approx 147yd/135m per 50g ball) in: 306 Begonia (A), 304 Orchid (B) and 301 Daisy (C)
- 2.5mm (UK12:USC/2) crochet hook
- Scissors
- Blunt-ended tapestry needle
- 2 pairs of jewellery pliers (including flat nose pliers)
- Side cutters
- Scrap of fabric
- 2 x 1¼in (3cm) ribbon clamps
- 2 x jumprings
- 1 x chain necklace, approx 18in (45cm) long
- Iron and damp cloth

Key

ᴑ	chain (ch)
+	Double crochet
✕✕	Dc2inc
⋀⋀	Dc2dec

SPECIAL ABBREVIATIONS

Dc2inc Work 2 dc into the same st to increase.
Dc2dc Work 2 dc together to decrease.

TENSION

4 sts and 24 rows to 10cm over double crochet on 2.5mm hook.

PATTERN

With 2.5mm hook and A, make 41 ch.
Row 1 (RS): 1 dc into second ch from hook, 1 dc into next 39 ch, turn (40 sts).
Row 2 (WS): 1 ch (does not count as a st), 1 dc into first dc, 1 dc into next 5 dc, *make 8 ch, 1 dc into second ch from hook, 1 dc into next 6 ch, 1 dc into next 7 dc; rep from * 3 more times, make 8 ch, 1 dc into second ch from hook, 1 dc into next 6 ch, 1 dc into next 6 dc, turn.
Join and continue in B.
Row 3: 1 ch (does not count as a st), 1 dc into first dc, 1 dc into next 4 dc, *dc2dec, 1 dc into next 5 dc, work 2 dc into next dc, miss turning ch, 2 dc into reverse side of next ch, 1 dc into reverse side of next 5 ch, dc2dec, 1 dc into next 5 dc; rep from * 4 more times, turn.
Row 4: 1 ch (does not count as a st), 1 dc into first dc, *1 dc into next 3 dc, dc2dec, 1 dc into next 6 dc, (dc2inc) twice, 1 dc into next 6 dc, dc2dec; rep from * 4 more times, 1 dc into next 4 dc, turn.
Row 5: 1 ch (does not count as a st), 1 dc into first 2 dc, *1 dc into next dc, dc2dec, 1 dc into next 6 dc, dc2inc, 1 dc into next 2 dc, dc2inc, 1 dc into next 6 dc, dc2dec; rep from * 4 times, 1 dc into next 3 dc, turn.
Row 6: 1 ch (does not count as a st), 1 dc into first 2 dc, * miss next dc, dc2dec, 1 dc into next 6 dc, dc2inc, 1 dc into next 2 dc, dc2inc, 1 dc into next 6 dc, dc2dec; rep from * 4 times, miss next dc, 1 dc into next 2 dc, turn.
Join and continue in C.
Row 7: 1 ch (does not count as a st), 1 dc into first 2 dc, *dc2dec, 1 dc into next 6 dc, dc2inc, 1 dc into next 2 dc, dc2inc, 1 dc into next 6 dc, dc2dec; rep from * 4 times, 1 dc into next 2 dc.
Fasten off.

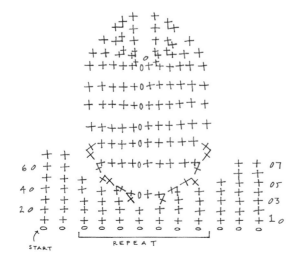

TO MAKE UP THE NECKLACE

1 Weave in the ends using a blunt-ended tapestry needle, threading them through the stitches at the sides of the work as this will be hidden inside the ribbon clamps. Press the work under a damp cloth (**image 1**).

2 Carefully insert one end of the crocheted piece inside a ribbon clamp, using the point of the scissors to help ease it in. Take care not to snag the yarn on the teeth of the clamps.

3 Place a scrap of folded fabric over the clamp and, with the flat nose pliers, squeeze the sides of it together to encase the work (**image 2**). Be careful not to catch the fabric in the ribbon clamp.

4 Use the cutters to cut the chain in two equal lengths. Each length of chain can be cut down to make a shorter necklace, if preferred.

5 Open up a jumpring by gripping each end with a pair of pliers and easing the wire apart. Thread through the loop in the ribbon clamp. Thread the end chain of one half of the necklace onto the jumpring and, holding the ring with one pair of pliers, use the other pair to close the jumpring. Repeat to attach the other half of the chain to the loop on the other ribbon clamp to finish the necklace (**image 3**).

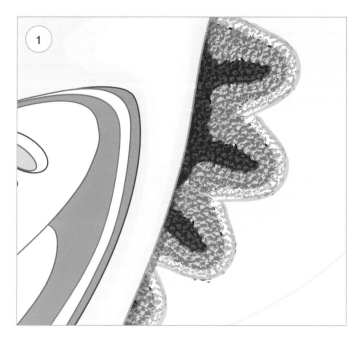

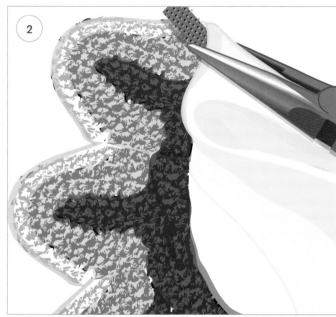

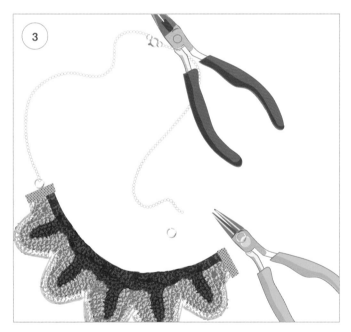

Granny Squares Purse

Crocheted patches make a pretty lined purse to complement your summer wardrobe. Tension is important here so make sure you crochet a swatch before embarking on this project.

MATERIALS

- Rowan wool cotton 4-ply, 50% merino wool, 50% cotton (approx 196yd/180m per 50g ball) in: 487 Aqua (A), 492 Sea (B), 484 Petal (C), 485 Flower (D), 491 Leaf (E), 488 Butter (F)
- 2.5mm (UK12/USC/2) crochet hook
- Approx 16 x 8in (40 x 20cm) each of plain and patterned fabric
- Sewing thread to match fabric
- Sewing machine
- Sewing needle
- Tapestry needle
- Approx 6in (15cm) purse frame
- Fabric glue

TENSION
6 sets of 3 tr and 1ch and 10 rows of treble stitches to 4in (10cm) on 2.5mm hook.
Use larger or smaller hook if necessary to obtain correct tension.

SPECIAL ABBREVIATION
3trcl (3 treble cluster): Yarn round hook, insert hook into next st, catch yarn and draw back through st (3 loops on hook), catch yarn again and draw through 2 loops (2 loops on hook), *yrh, insert hook into same st, catch yarn and draw back through st (4 loops on hook), catch yarn and draw through 2 loops* (3 loops on hook), repeat from * to * once more (4 loops on hook), yrh, draw through all 4 loops.

CIRCLE IN A SQUARE PATCH

With 2.5mm hook and A, make 6 ch and sl st to first ch to form a ring.

Round 1: 3 ch to count as first tr, 1 tr into the ring, 1 ch, (2 tr into ring, 1 ch) 5 times, sl st to the third of 3 ch (6 sets of 2 tr).

Round 2: Sl st into next st, sl st into next 1 ch sp, 3 ch to count as first tr, (1 tr, 1 ch, 2 tr, 1 ch) into the same 1 ch sp, (2 tr, 1 ch) twice into each of the next five 1 ch sps, sl st to third of 3 ch (12 sets of 2 tr).

Round 3: Sl st into next st, sl st into next 1 ch sp, 3 ch to count as first tr, 2 tr into the same 1 ch sp, 1 ch, (3 tr into next 1 ch sp, 1 ch) 11 times, sl st to third of 3 ch (12 sets of 3 tr).

Round 4: Sl st into next st, work as for Round 3. Fasten off. Join in B to the first 1 ch sp with a sl st (**image 1**).

Round 5: 3 ch to count as first tr, (2 tr, 1 ch, 3 tr) into the same 1 ch sp, 1 ch, (3 tr, 1 ch) twice into each of the next eleven 1 ch sps, sl st to third of 3 ch (24 sets of 3 tr). Fasten off. Join in C to the first 1 ch sp with a sl st.

Round 6: 3 ch to count as first tr, 2 tr into the same 1 ch sp, 1 ch, (3 tr into next 1 ch sp, 1 ch) 23 times (24 sets of 3 tr). Sl st to third of 3 ch. Fasten off. Join in D to the first 1 ch sp with a sl st.

Round 7: 3 ch to count as first tr, 2 tr in same 1 ch sp, *1 ch, 3 htr in next 1 ch sp, 1 ch (2 dc in next 1 ch sp, 1 ch) 3 times, 3 htr in next 1 ch sp, 1 ch, (3 tr, 2 ch, 3 tr) in next 1 ch sp to create corner (**image 2**); rep from * twice more, 1 ch, 3 htr in next 1 ch sp, 1 ch (2 dc in next 1 ch sp, 1 ch) 3 times, 3 htr in next 1 ch sp, 1 ch, 3 tr into same 1 ch sp as beginning of round, 2 ch, sl st into third of 3 ch.

Round 8: Sl st into the 2 ch sp at the corner, 3 ch to count as first tr, 2 tr in same 2 ch sp, *1 ch, (3 tr in next 1 ch sp, 1 ch) 6 times, (3 tr, 2 ch, 3 tr) in next 2 ch sp; rep from * twice more, 1 ch, (3 tr, in next 1 ch sp, 1 ch) 6 times, 3 tr into same 2 ch sp as beginning of round, 2 ch, sl st to third of 3 ch (32 sets of 3 tr).

Round 9: Sl st into the 2 ch sp at the corner, 3 ch to count as first tr, 2 tr in same 2 ch sp, *1 ch, (3 tr in next 1 ch sp, 1 ch) 7 times, (3 tr, 2 ch, 3 tr) in next 2 ch sp; rep from * twice more, 1 ch, (3 tr, in next 1 ch sp, 1 ch) 7 times, 3 tr into same 2 ch sp as beginning of round, 2 ch, sl st to third of 3 ch (36 sets of 3 tr). Fasten off. Make one more patch to match the first.

SMALL MULTI PATCHWORK

With 2.5mm hook and A, B, C, D or F, make 6 ch and join with a sl st to the first ch to form a ring.

Round 1: Work as for the Circle in a Square Patch (6 sets of 2 tr). Fasten off. Join E to the first 1 ch sp with a sl st.

Round 2: 3 ch to count as first tr, (1 tr, 1 ch, 2 tr, 1 ch) into the same 1 ch sp, (2 tr, 1 ch) twice into each of the next five 1 ch sps, sl st to third of 3 ch (12 sets of 2 tr).

Round 3: Sl st to next st, sl st into next 1 ch sp, 3 ch to count as

first tr, 1 tr in the same 1 ch sp, * 1 ch, (2 htr in next 1 ch sp, 1 ch) twice, (2 tr, 2 ch, 2 tr) in next 1 ch sp to form a corner; rep from * twice more, 1 ch, (2 htr in next 1 ch sp, 1 ch) twice, 2 tr into same 1 ch sp as beginning of round, 2 ch, sl st to the third of 3 ch. Fasten off.

Make 17 more patches.

Weave in the yarn ends.

Lay the 9 patches out for each side of the purse in the order you would like them.

Join C to corner of first patch with a sl st.

Next: With WS together, 2.5mm hook and C, work 1 dc into back loops only of the 13 stitches along one edge of both pieces at the same time to join.

Do not fasten off, but continue working down the next two sets of patches in the same way to join two rows of patches. Fasten off.

Next: Repeat to join the remaining three patches.

Next: Rejoin C to the corner of a row to be joined across the patch with a sl st.

Work 1 dc into the back loops only of the 39 stitches along the edges of both pieces of each patch at the same time to join. Fasten off.

Next: Repeat to join the remaining row of one side of the purse (**image 3**).

Next: Rejoin C to a corner with a sl st, 1 dc into the back loop only of each st, sl st to first dc (156 sts).

Fasten off. Repeat to finish the other side.

Weave in the ends.

FLOWER PATCH

With 2.5mm hook and F, make 6 ch and sl st to first ch to form a ring.

Round 1: 1 ch, work 16 dc into the ring, sl st to the first dc (16 sts).

Round 2: 6 ch, miss 1 dc, (1 tr in next dc, 3 ch, miss 1 dc) 7 times, sl st to third of 6 ch (8 sps). Fasten off.

Join in C to the first 3 ch sp with a sl st.

Round 3: (In the next 3 ch sp work 1 dc, 1 htr, 3 tr, 1 htr, 1 dc) 8 times, sl st to first dc (8 petals). Fasten off.

Join in D between the first and the last dc with a sl st.

Round 4: Work 1 dc in the same sp, 6 ch, (1 dc between the next 2 dc, 6 ch) 7 times, sl st to first dc (8 spaces).

Round 5: 1 ch, (in the next 6 ch sp work 1 dc, 1 htr, 6 tr, 1 htr, 1 dc) 8 times, sl st to first dc (8 petals).

Fasten off.

Join in E to the middle of the first petal with a sl st (**image 4**).

Round 6: 1 dc in same st, *6 ch, (3trcl, 4 ch, 3trcl) into the middle of the next petal (**image 5**), 6 ch, 1 dc in middle of next petal; rep from * 2 more times, 6 ch, (3trcl, 4 ch, 3trcl) into the middle of the next petal, 6 ch, sl st into first dc.

Fasten off.

Join B into a 4 ch corner sp with a sl st.

Round 7: 3 ch to count as first tr, 2 tr in same 4 ch sp, 1 ch, *(3 tr, 1 ch) twice into each of next two 6 ch sps, (3 tr, 2 ch, 3 tr) into next 4 ch corner sp, 1 ch; rep from * twice more, (3 tr, 1 ch) twice

into each of next two 6 ch sps, 3 tr into same 4 ch sp as beginning of round, 2 ch, sl st to third of 3 ch (24 sets of 3 tr). Fasten off.

Join A into a 2 ch corner sp with a sl st.

Round 8: 3 ch to count as first tr, 2 tr in same 2 ch sp, 1 ch, *(3 tr in next 1 ch sp, 1 ch) 5 times, (3 tr, 2 ch, 3 tr) in next 2 ch sp, 1 ch; rep from * twice more, (3 tr in next 1 ch sp, 1 ch) 5 times, 3 tr into same 2 ch sp as beginning of round, 2 ch, sl st to third of 3 ch (28 sets of 3 tr).

Round 9: Work as for Round 8 of the Circle in a Square patch.

Round 10: Work as for Round 9 of the Circle in a Square patch.

Fasten off.

Make one more patch to match the first.

TO FINISH

Weave in the ends and press the patches with a warm iron under a damp cloth.

To join the circle in a square and flower patches

With RS together, miss the 2 ch sp and 3 tr at the corner, miss next 2 sets of 3 tr and rejoin yarn last used to back loop of next tr with

a sl st. Working into back loops only on both sides at the same time to join, 1 dc in the same tr, 1 dc in next 2 tr, (1 dc in next ch, 1 dc in next 3 tr) 5 times, 2 dc in each of next 2 ch at corner, (1 dc in next 3 tr, 1 dc in next ch) 8 times, 1 dc in next 3 tr, 2 dc in each of next 2 ch at corner, (1 dc in next 3 tr, 1 dc in next ch) 5 times, 1 dc in the next 3 tr, fasten off (**image 6**).
Fasten off and weave in the ends.

To join the multi patchwork pieces

With RS together, rejoin C to the side edge with a sl st in the first dc of the second patch. Working into both sides at the same time to join, 1 dc into back loops of the first and the next 24 dc, 2 dc in each of next 2 dc at the corner, 1 dc in the next 37 dc along lower edge, 2 dc in each of next 2 dc at the corner, 1 dc in next 25 dc (**image 7**). Fasten off and weave in the ends.

To make the lining

1 Cut two pieces of fabric each in printed and plain from the lining pattern. Stitch a ⅜in (1cm) seam between the dots to join lower and side edges. Cut diagonally across the corners.

2 With RS together, slip one piece of fabric inside the other, aligning the raw edges at the top and sides. Working on one side at a time, stitch the two pieces of the lining together around the curved top edges between the dots, allowing a ⅜in (1cm) seam. Leave an opening of around 5cm on one top edge to turn the piece right side out. Notch the curves (**image 8**).

3 Turn the lining RS out and press. Sew the opening together by hand or machine. This way, the raw edges are inside the lining and won't show through the open work of the crocheted patches.

4 With the patterned side on the inside, insert the lining into the crocheted purse. Line up the curved edges and pin in place. Sew by hand or machine around the open edges to attach the crocheted piece to the lining (**image 9**).

5 Working on one side at a time, apply the glue to the channel of one side of the purse frame, coating the base and sides. Carefully insert the top of the lined crochet and allow the glue to dry. Repeat to attach the other side of the purse frame.

GRANNY SQUARES PURSE TEMPLATE AND CHARTS

TOP ⅜in (1cm) seam

Purse lining
Cut 2 in plain fabric
Cut 2 in patterned fabric

⅜in (1cm)

⅜in (1cm)

Enlarge to 125% for actual size

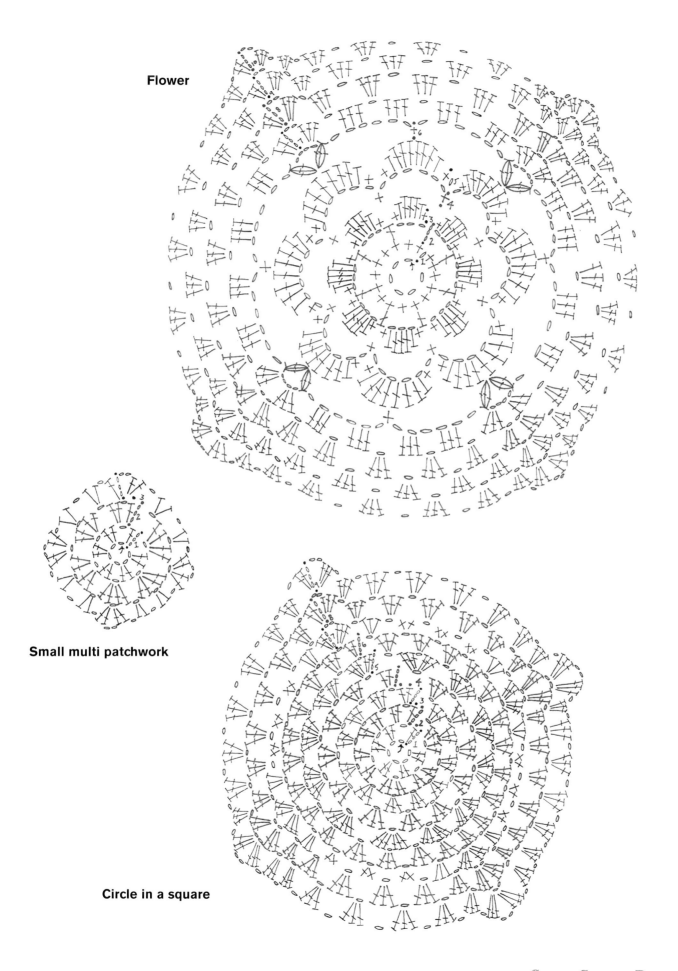

Flower

Small multi patchwork

Circle in a square

Votive Covers

MATERIALS

- Fine (3-ply) crochet cotton thread in your main colour (A)
- Approx 40in (1m) of a contrast colour (B)
- 2mm (UK14:USB/1) crochet hook
- Scissors
- Embroidery needle
- Glass votive

A sweet gift or a nice handmade touch for your own home, these crochet covers add warmth to glass tea light votives. These glass votives are approximately 2½in (6cm) in diameter and 2¾in (7cm) high.

Using 2mm hook and A, 5 ch, sl st into first ch to join and form a ring (6 sts).

Round 1: 3 ch (counts as first tr), tr 11, sl st into third ch of first 3 ch to join (12 sts).

Round 2: 2 ch (counts as first dc), dc 2 into next st 11 times, dc into base of first 2 ch, sl st into second st of first 2 ch to join (24 sts).

Round 3: 3 ch (counts as first tr), tr 2 into next st and following 22 sts, tr 1 into base of first 3 ch, sl st into third ch of first 3 ch to join (48 sts).

Round 4: 2 ch, *dc 1 into next st, dc 2 into next st, rep from * until last st before first 2 ch, sl st in second ch of 2 ch to join (72 sts).

Round 5: 2 ch, dc in every st, sl st in second ch of 2 ch to join (72 sts).

Round 6: 3 ch, tr in every st, sl st in third ch of 3 ch to join (72 sts).

Rounds 7–11: As Round 5.

Round 12: As Round 6.

Round 13 onwards: As Round 5 until you reach the desired length.

Final Round: Change to B and work as Round 5.

Cut yarn to 2½in (5cm) and pull through last loop with hook. Use an embroidery needle to weave your thread in.

Boho Chic Shopper

Make an on-trend shopping bag using fun and colourful crochet granny squares.

MATERIALS

- Rowan Kid Classic 70% lambswool, 22%, kid mohair, 8% polyamide (approx 153yd/140m per 50g ball):
  1 x ball in 841 Lavender Ice (A)
  1 x ball in 828 Feather (B)
  1 x ball in 886 Grasshopper (C)
  1 x ball in 877 Mellow (D)
  1 x ball in 852 Victoria (E)
  1 x ball in 887 Grape (F)
  1 x ball in 885 Cloudy (G)
  1 x ball in 871 Canard (H)
  1 x ball in 866 Bitter Sweet (I)
  1 x ball in 882 Lime (J)
- 4mm (UK8:USG/6) crochet hook
- 1 pair of 7in (18cm) diameter bamboo handles
- Approx 22 x 14in (55 x 35cm) fabric for inner lining
- Approx 22 x 14in (55 x 35cm) fabric for inner lining

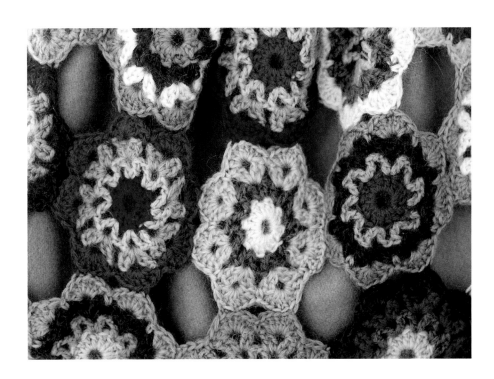

SIZE

Finished bag is approx 20in (50cm) at widest point and 11in (28cm) at deepest point.

BASIC MOTIF

Make 6 ch, join with sl st to form a ring.

Round 1: 3 ch (counts as 1 tr), work 15 tr into ring, join with sl st to third of 3 ch (16 tr)..

Round 2: 5 ch (counts as tr, 2 ch), 1 tr into same st as last sl st, *1 ch, miss 1 tr, (1 tr, 2 ch, 1 tr) into next tr; rep from * 6 more times, 1 ch, join with sl st to third of 5 ch.

Round 3: Sl st into first 2 ch sp, 3 ch (counts as 1 tr), (1 tr, 2 ch, 2 tr) into same sp, *1 ch, (2 tr, 2 ch, 2 tr) into next 2 ch sp; rep from * 6 more times, 1 ch, join with sl st to third of 3 ch.

Round 4: Sl st into next tr and first 2 ch sp, 3 ch, 6 tr into same sp as last sl st, 1 dc into next ch sp, (7 tr into next 2 ch sp, 1 dc into next ch sp) 6 more times, join with sl st to third of 3 ch.
Fasten off.

BAG

Make 2 of each motif, one for the front and one for the back.
Colour sequences for top row from left to right:
ABCD, CEBA, HGDF, EJIB, GFHJ.
Colour sequences for middle row from left to right:
BJAE, FGDH, BIJG, HDEA, FABD.
Colour sequences for bottom row from left to right:
DFGC, GCED, EDAC, JIHE, BCFG.
Weave in any loose ends and press the work according to ball band instructions.

Join motifs by slip stitching the centre 3 trebles of two of the petal points to corresponding petal points of next motif until you have joined all the petals in the colour sequence as set.

Rep for other side and then join base and sides in the same way.

HANDLE COVER

Join yarn D to second of 7 tr of top RH motif.

Row 1 (RS): 1 ch, 1 dc in same place, 1 dc in next 4 tr, 1 dc in centre 5 tr of each petal point to end of row, turn (50 dc).

Row 2: 1 ch, 1 dc in every dc to end of row.

Repeat Row 2 fifteen more times.

Fasten off. Repeat for other side.

TO FINISH OFF

Inner lining

Place right sides of fabric together and stitch together, leaving a ⅝in (1.5cm) seam allowance for the sides and a ⅜in (1cm) seam allowance for the base. Press out seams.

Outer lining

Place right sides of fabric together and stitch together, leaving a ⅝in (1.5cm) seam allowance for the sides and a ⅜in (1cm) seam allowance for the base. Press out seams. Place inner lining inside outer lining so that wrong sides are together.

Fold inner lining over the top of outer lining to form a hem and top stitch into place.

Place linings inside crochet shell, turn work inside out and stitch top of lining into place, easing and gathering slightly where necessary.

Place hoop handle inside crocheted cover and slipstitch into place. Repeat for other handle.

Turn work right side out.

> **TIP**
> This bag would work equally well with a random selection of yarns, but keep to the same yarn weight.

Techniques

Getting started

Here is the basic information you will need, from how to hold the hook and yarn, to crocheting the various stitches. Before you start your project, check through the list of materials at the beginning of each pattern and gather together everything you will need.

HOOKS

Crochet hooks come in a range of sizes, which correspond to the weight (thickness) of the yarn. Tiny hooks are used on very fine yarns, chunky weight yarns require a much thicker hook. Using a larger or smaller hook will change the look of the fabric and will also affect the tension and the amount of yarn required. The ball band on a ball of yarn will have information on the suggested size of hook for that yarn. Hooks come in materials including plastic, steel, aluminium, bamboo and crochet. A good-quality hook is easier to push through the stitches and helps you work faster and with a more even tension.

NEEDLES

You will need a blunt-ended tapestry needle to sew the projects together. The large eye makes it easy to thread the needle with thick yarns and the rounded end will prevent any snagging.

YARN

It is a good idea to choose a yarn that is colourfast. Choose a yarn with a firm twist that is less likely to unravel during the process. It is relatively simple to substitute the yarns recommended for the projects in this book if it is difficult to source or you have something in your stash that you want to use up.

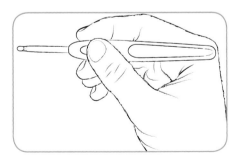

HOLDING THE HOOK

Hold the hook in either your right or left hand as you would a pencil, in between your index finger and thumb, about 1¼–2in (3–5cm) from the hook end. If your hook has a flat handle then hold it there for comfort.

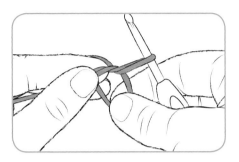

MAKING A SLIP KNOT

Crochet starts by forming a slip knot, which is easy to tighten or loosen on your crochet hook. Make a loop of yarn over two fingers. Pull a second loop through this first loop. Pull up the loop and slip this loop onto your crochet hook. Pull both ends of the yarn to gently tighten the knot on the hook.

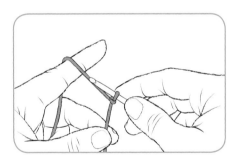

HOLDING THE YARN

When you hold the yarn, the most important consideration is to create some tension between the yarn and the crochet hook. This will make it easier and quicker to wrap your yarn around the hook when making a stitch. Unwind a length of yarn from the ball. Wrap the end of the yarn around the little finger of the hand not holding the crochet hook, pass the yarn under your middle and ring fingers and then bring the yarn up and over your forefinger. Hold the chain or crochet fabric steady between the middle finger and thumb of the same hand. Raise your forefinger when you want to increase the tension in the yarn.

Crochet know-how

CHAIN STITCH (ch)

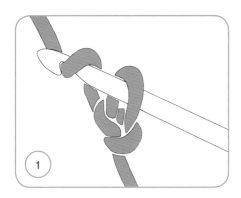

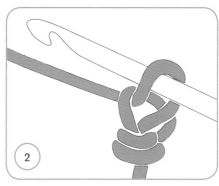

1 With hook in right hand and yarn resting over middle finger of left hand, pull yarn taut. Take hook under then over yarn.

2 Pull the hook and yarn through the loop while holding slip knot steady.

Repeat this process to form a foundation row of chain stitch.

SLIP STITCH (sl st)

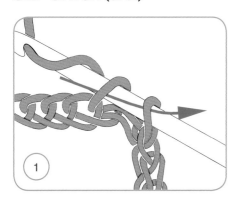

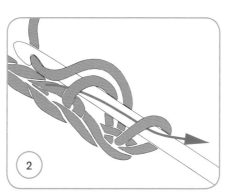

1 Slip the hook under the top two strands of the 'V' of the first stitch of the row.

2 Wrap yarn around hook and draw it back through both the 'V' and the loop on the hook.

DOUBLE CROCHET (dc)

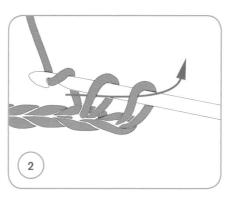

1 Start by placing hook into a stitch. Wrap new yarn round the hook and draw loop back through work towards you. There should now be two loops on the hook.

2 Wrap the yarn around hook once more, then draw through both loops. There should now be one loop left on the hook. One double crochet stitch is now complete. Repeat as required.

HALF TREBLE (htr)

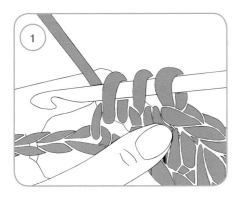 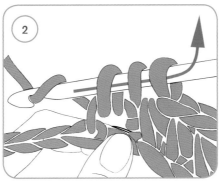

1 Wrap yarn around hook and place into a stitch. Wrap yarn around hook and then draw the loop through. There should now be three loops on the hook.

2 Wrap yarn around hook again and draw through the three loops. There should be one loop left on the hook.

TREBLE CROCHET (tr)

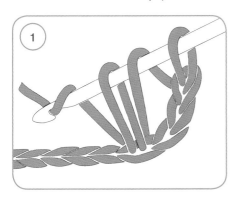 

Follow instructions for half treble until there are three loops on the hook.

1 Catch the yarn with hook and draw through two of the loops.

2 Catch yarn again and draw it through the remaining two loops.

DOUBLE TREBLE (dtr)

Follow instructions for half treble until there are three loops on the hook.

1 Wrap yarn around hook twice and then place into a stitch.

2 Wrap yarn around hook and then draw the loop through (four loops should now be on hook).

3 Catch the yarn and draw through two of the loops.

4 Catch yarn again and draw it through two loops.

5 Catch the yarn once more and draw through the remaining two loops.

MAGIC CIRCLE

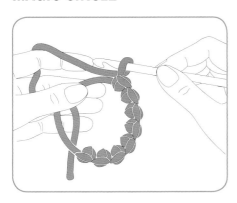

Use a magic circle to make a very tight centre.

1 Make a half-formed slip knot.

2 Make all the first-round stitches into the circle.

3 Pull the end tight after completing one round.

TIP
When you start a new ball of yarn, leave a tail of at least 6in (15cm) instead of a fiddly short tail that would be difficult to thread through a needle when it comes to weaving in the ends.

CHANGING COLOURS

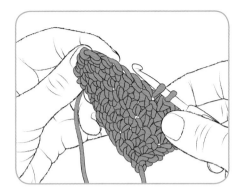

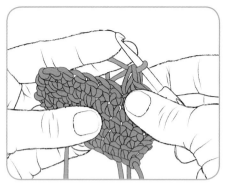

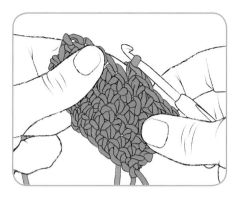

1 Crochet to the point where there are two loops of the last stitch before the colour change.

2 Drop the old colour, wrap the new colour of yarn over the hook and pull this new colour through both loops of the first colour.

3 Using the second colour of yarn, you can now dc into the next stitch as usual.

FASTENING OFF

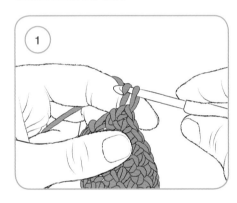

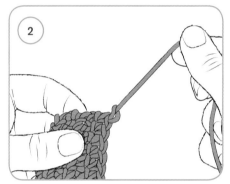

1 When you have finished your crochet, pull the last stitch through the loop on your hook.

2 Cut the yarn, leaving a 6in (15cm) tail, then thread this through the centre of the loop and pull tightly to form a small knot.

WEAVING IN ENDS

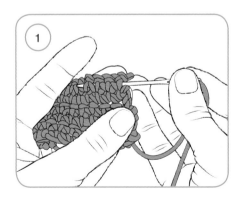

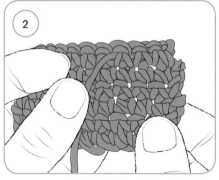

1 Thread the remaining yarn end onto a blunt tapestry needle and weave in the yarn on the wrong side of the project. Work along the stitches one way and then back in the opposite direction.

2 Weave the needle behind the first ridge of crochet for at least 2in (5cm). Snip off the end of the yarn closely to the fabric of the crochet.

Sewing Up

SEWING UP

When stitching up your work, use safety pins or glass-headed dressmaker's pins to hold the pieces together. Here are different ways that can be used to finish off the crocheted projects.

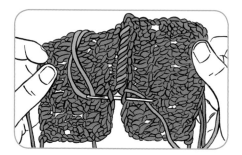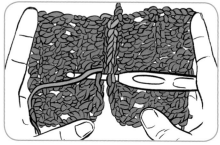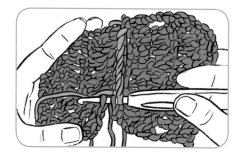

WHIP STITCH

Use a whip stitch if you want to sew your seams together. Place the two pieces of crochet wrong sides together and push your needle through both pieces. Repeat evenly along the edge. There will be a row of small stitches along the edge of your work, joining both pieces together.

SLIP-STITCH SEAM

A slip-stitch seam is a neat and strong way of attaching crochet pieces together. Place the crochet pieces together. Insert the hook through both edge stitches, yarn over hook, pull up a loop and chain one stitch. Work a row of slip stitches by inserting your hook through both sides at the same time. Keep the work fairly loose.

DOUBLE-CROCHET SEAM

A double-crochet seam is useful for joining two straight edges together. It can be worked on the right side of the work and used as a decorative edge. Place two pieces of crochet together, either with the right sides or wrong sides together. Insert the hook through both edge stitches, yarn over hook, pull up a loop and then work one double-crochet stitch. Then work in double crochet as usual along the edge. If you work around a corner, work three dc into the corner stitch.

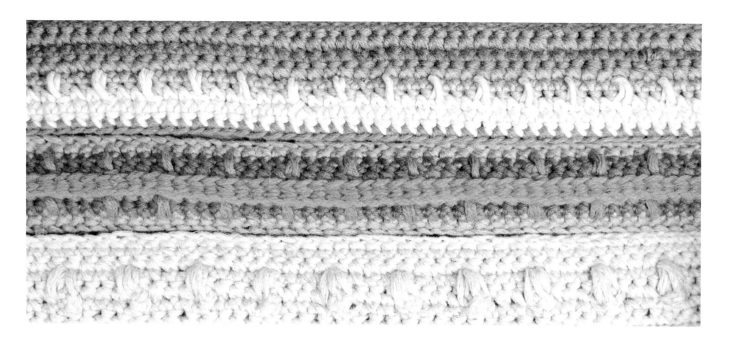

Abbreviations

Conversions

ABBREVIATIONS

approx	approximately
ch	chain
cm	centimetre(s)
cont	continue
dc	double crochet
dc2dec	work 2 dc sts together to decrease
dc2inc	work 2 dc sts into the next st to increase
dc3inc	work 3 dc sts into the next st to increase
dec	decrease
dtr	double treble
htr	half treble
in	inch(es)
inc	increase
m	metre(s)
mm	millimetre(s)
rep	repeat
RS	right side
sl st	slip stitch
sp	space
st(s)	stitch(es)
tr	treble
tr3inc	work 3 tr sts into the next st to increase
trtr	triple treble
WS	wrong side
yd	yard(s)
yrh	yarn round hook

CROCHET HOOK SIZES

UK	Metric	US
14	2mm	B/1
12	2.5mm	C/2
11	3mm	–
10	3.25mm	D/3
9	3.5mm	E/4
8	4mm	G/6
7	4.5mm	7
6	5mm	H/8

UK/US YARN WEIGHTS

UK	US
2-ply	Lace
3-ply	Fingering
4-ply	Sport
Double knitting (DK)	Light worsted
Aran	Fisherman/worsted
Chunky	Bulky
Super chunky	Extra bulky

UK/US CROCHET TERMS

UK	US
Double crochet	Single crochet
Half treble	Half double crochet
Treble	Double crochet
Double treble	Triple crochet

NOTE: This booklet uses UK crochet techniques.